# LEGENDS OF MARYLAND BASKETBALL

DAVE UNGRADY

www.SportsPublishingLLC.com

ISBN: 1-58261-805-4

Publishers: Peter L. Bannon and Joseph Bannon Sr.
Senior managing editor: Susan M. Moyer
Acquisitions editor: Dean Reinke
Developmental editor: Doug Hoepker
Art director: K. Jeffrey Higgerson
Book design: Heidi Norsen
Dust jacket design: Heidi Norsen
Project manager: Jim Henehan
Imaging: Kenneth J. O'Brien, Dustin Hubbart, Heidi Norsen and
        Christine Mohrbacher
Photo editor: Erin Linden-Levy
Vice president of sales and marketing: Kevin King
Media and promotions managers:
        Courtney Hainline (regional marketing manager)
        Randy Fouts (national marketing manager)
        Maurey Williamson (print marketing manager)

Printed in the United States

Sports Publishing L.L.C.
804 North Neil Street
Champaign, IL 61820

Phone: 1-877-424-2665
Fax: 217-363-2073
Web site: www.SportsPublishingLLC.com

*To my former Maryland teammates and coaches*
*with the soccer team ('76) and the track team ('76-'80),*
*thanks for the memories, the leadership and the continued friendships.*

# CONTENTS

renewals and many joined the association for the first time. Financial contributions for the entire university have increased greatly for each of the past three years.

Many of Williams's former athletes, including most of the legends cited in this book, are seen at games in the Comcast Center and around the nation wherever the Terps may be playing. His basketball team charters a plane for all trips, where it is feasible, in order for the team to return home immediately following the game and be in class the next morning.

When Charles "Lefty" Driesell moved onto the basketball scene in Cole Field House, he decided his first move was to entice fans to come to the games and see the best players he could recruit. He began by winning over the student body, flashing a V sign when he entered the court, and moving students down onto the floor closer to the action.

The student band played "Hail to the Chief" as he entered. He later requested that they drop this from their repertoire. He also campaigned to have the ACC Tournament moved around the league as it had always been played in the state of North Carolina. He vowed that when he won his first title he would bolt the trophy to the hood of his car and drive all around North Carolina. Lefty was in the title game five times before sweeping the tournament in 1984. Due to the NCAA tournament, Lefty did not have time to take his joy ride through North Carolina.

During the 1970-71 season, Driesell's second year as Maryland coach, the South Carolina Gamecocks came to Cole ranked second in the nation. An earlier game between the two that year at South Carolina featured an altercation that resulted in a bruised chin for the lefthander. The Gamecocks had scored 96 points in the game in Columbia that was terminated with four minutes remaining.

In the game in College Park, South Carolina trailed 4-3 at the half and lost 31-30 in overtime. Jim O'Brien scored with five seconds left in regulation and then hit the winner with four seconds remaining in overtime.

Albert King was voted ACC Player of the Year in 1980 and All-America in 1980 and 1981. He scored in double figures all four years at Maryland. However, in 1980 following a 73-72 loss to Duke, King was voted the MVP of the ACC tournament, but could not be found to accept the award on the court. After searching the locker room and surrounding area, I found him sitting in the back corner of the shower, with his head down and tears in his eyes. It required considerable persuasion to lure him from the shower room back onto the court. Both of us, slightly dampened, returned to the court and as he came out of the tunnel he received a standing ovation from the Duke and Terrapin fans for his performance.

Chris Weller developed a number of All-Americans in the women's program, including Tara Heiss and Vicky Bullett, both cited in this book. However, it was Dottie McKnight who served as the first coach of women's basketball under the auspices of the Department of Intercollegiate Athletics in Cole Field House. McKnight had coached the team for six years in Prinkert Field House. She moved to Cole Field House in 1971 when the team became a varsity squad and compiled a 44-17 record in four years, winning two state championships. McKnight turned the program over to one of her former players, Weller, in 1975.

In 1971 many women's coaches did not believe in putting numbers on players or over-publicizing them. Of course, not realizing this in 1974, I arranged for Monica Rogers to have a one-on-one contest with local ABC sportscaster Steve Bassett, while Coach McKnight was out of town. The contest was split into two segments on the evening newscast. Monica defeated the sportscaster with a 15-foot jump shot. As he fell to the floor on his back, Monica walked over, placed her foot on his chest and pumped her fist into the air. The women's fans loved it, and I retired from Maryland before ever discussing it with Coach McKnight.

Working with sports at Maryland has been more a passion than a job. While at Maryland, I helped host two NCAA Final Four Championships in men's basketball. It was a thrill watching Texas Western and UCLA win NCAA basketball titles in Cole Field House.

I also worked a football game with the Queen of England in the stands, the opening and closing of Cole Field House and the opening of the Comcast Center. It all contributed to a great career at Maryland.

*Jack Zane retired from the Maryland athletic department in 2003. Before leaving, he directed the development of Maryland's Walk of Fame and History in the Comcast Center, a monumental tribute to Maryland's finest athletes. He is still an active member of the Maryland's alumni association, and he and his wife, Judy, are longtime members of the Terrapin Club, Building Partners in the Comcast Center and season ticket holders for both the men's and women's basketball teams, as well as football.*

*—Jack Zane*

# LEGENDS OF MARYLAND BASKETBALL

# BOSEY
# BERGER

# BURTON
# SHIPLEY

**H.** Burton Shipley was Maryland's first basketball coach of prominence, but his legend extends beyond the hardwoods. He served as the football team's waterboy in 1896 and earned 16 varsity letters while attending the college from 1908 to 1914. He was also captain of the football, baseball and basketball teams.

Shipley claimed he was chosen captain of the basketball team because he played football. And it appears he approached both games with vigor.

"We had an old gym with two pillars in it and played most of our games ... in a Sunday School gymnasium," he said in the book, *Maryland Basketball: Red, White and Amen.* "We didn't have an out of bounds, and the walls had radiators in them, which you could bump your opponent into."

Shipley showcased his attacking attributes on the football field as Maryland's starting quarterback for three years. On the basketball court, he was strictly a defensive enforcer. As a back guard, he protected Maryland's basket and tried to shut down the opposing team's best player.

"I used to stomp my foot to distract 'em," said Shipley in *Red, White and Amen.* "I couldn't shoot. I was a terrible shot."

Shipley claims he learned about the long pass and the zone defense from University of Illinois basketball coach Ralph Jones while he studied first aid at the school. Later, he implemented the techniques while coaching at several different colleges, and shared the idea with former Maryland star athlete Curley Byrd, then Maryland's athletic director and head basketball coach. Byrd liked the idea.

## BURTON SHIPLEY

**Years coached:** 1923-24 to 1946-47
**Record:** 243-199
**Career highlights:**
 Southern Conference tournament champion, 1930-31; Southern Conference regular season co-champion, 1931-32

"I came back to Maryland a little while later, and the players told me that Byrd had really thought up something good, a zone," Shipley said in *Red, White and Amen.*

Byrd rewarded Shipley for his innovative ways, selecting him as Maryland's new head basketball coach in 1923. He went on to coach Maryland for 24 seasons, still the longest of any coach in the history of the program.

# "His sense of humor stimulates all those with whom he associates on campus."

[BALTIMORE SUN]

The 1923-24 team was considered the school's first varsity team for the sport. The team started playing its games that year in a new facility called The Gymnasium, located in Annapolis Hall on the south part of campus.

It took just two seasons for Shipley to fashion his first winning season. Maryland quickly established itself as a prominent Southern Conference team, finishing in fourth place in the 1925 and 1926 seasons, and in third place in the 1928 season. A few years later, Maryland reached the pinnacle of Shipley's coaching career.

The 1930-31 season started ominously for Maryland. Because so many basketball players played football for Maryland, the team did not start practice until after Christmas, after every other area team had already started practicing. Also, the team's leading scorer the previous season, Bob Wilson, quit school, reducing the roster to eight players.

But six other players returned to the team. Bosey Berger was the most prized possession. Berger was a two-time basketball All-American at Maryland and is considered one of Maryland's all-time greatest athletes. Berger, a 6-2 forward, was considered one of the team's best shooters.

Maryland compiled its best regular-season record to date, 14-4, and then went on to win its first Southern Conference tournament title. They ended the year with Shipley's best record, 18-4. The next season, Maryland finished 16-4 and was Southern Conference regular-season co-champions.

Shipley completed his 24 seasons as Maryland coach with a 243-199 record. The "Ship" was equally renowned for his colorful personality. "His sense of humor stimulates all those with whom he associates on campus," wrote the *Baltimore Sun* in 1951.

A fan once hit him in the head with a water bag.

"I remember a time they got rowdy during one game," said Shipley, in *Maryland Basketball: Red, White and Amen.*

"Things weren't going so well. Somebody yelled through the quiet, 'Do Somethin', Ship!'"

Shipley's daughter later named a race-horse after the expression.

Late in his career as Maryland basketball coach, Shipley chased Tommy Mont into the locker room after the player made a mistake that cost the team a game. The players led him in to the shower and turned the water on the coach, saying, "You're all wet, Ship."

After Shipley was ejected from his final game as Maryland's baseball coach, he sat down on a chair outside the dugout and refused to leave the field. The umpire let him remain in the stadium that still bears his name.

Shipley coached his last team at Maryland in 1960, leaving behind one of the more compelling athletic careers at Maryland.

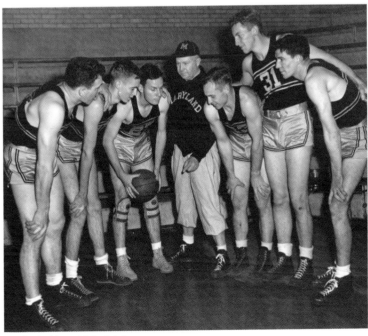

Maryland Athletics, Media Relations

# GENE
# SHUE

Gene Shue entered the University of Maryland when a basketball revolution was beginning in College Park, compliments of new head coach Bud Millikan. Before Millikan began his 17-year career with the Terps in 1950, Maryland basketball recorded a winning season just one time in the previous 10 years. Millikan completed his first year as head coach in 1951 with a 16-11 record. That year, Shue was developing into a future player of prominence with Maryland's freshman team, a player who would jump start Maryland basketball's second generation of conference contention and national respectability.

Before he took his first jump shot in College Park, it seemed Shue was an unlikely savior of a program gone bad. Shue was considered too small for basketball when he entered Towson Catholic High School in Baltimore only five foot three, prompting the nicknames "little mouse" and "bones."

But Shue turned out to be Millikan's most prized recruit during the coach's early years in the 1950s. A supporter of Maryland athletics informed Millikan about Shue's talents. During that time, recruits were able to take part in tryouts against other players, and Millikan said he saw right away that Shue was a hard worker with a lot of talent.

Several schools, mostly from the Baltimore-Washington area, recruited Shue out of high school. Shue wanted to attend Georgetown, but he struggled during two tryouts and Georgetown was waiting on a decision from another player. Millikan gave Shue 10 days to give him an answer. Shue accepted a deal at Maryland that required him to work odd jobs in his dormitory at

Ritchie Coliseum, where the Terps played their home games, and later sweep the floor of the coliseum in exchange for a scholarship. He earned a full scholarship his senior year.

"We used to come down and turn the lights on and play basketball late at night," said Shue. "Basketball was our life in those days."

Shue was considered a complete player, He was a sturdy rebounder and adept at the two-handed set shot. An emotionless demeanor belied his intensity. Millikan once called him a "deadpan performer" and said he exemplified the old athletic saying, "ice water in his veins."

He also defended the other team's best player. Maryland finished 13-9 during Shue's sophomore season, and finished the regular season in sixth place in the Southern Conference. The team's final loss came in the first round of the conference tournament, to 12th-ranked Duke. Less than one month prior to that game, Duke beat Maryland by five points. A Terps upset in the conference tournament was certainly conceivable.

Shue's assignment of guarding Dick Groat in those games created his most fond memories as a Terp. Shue called Groat

"everybody's All-American" for his prowess in basketball and baseball while at Duke. Groat later played both sports professionally, and in 1952 was an All-American, National Player of the Year and averaged 26 points per game during his senior season.

Shue, then a sophomore, was a bit taller than the six-foot Groat. But that didn't ease Shue's anxiety about defending the scoring machine.

"I was scared to death," said Shue. "Groat had such a huge reputation as a basketball player. Duke was a big rival. The whole atmosphere was unbelievable. I was a lowly sophomore. I know I did my best, whatever in the hell that was. My job was to put the clamps on people."

When the two teams met in the first round of the conference tournament at Reynolds Coliseum in Raleigh, Duke was enjoying a 13-game winning streak. Shue was

# BUD MILLIKAN

W hen Bud Millikan took over the Maryland basketball program in 1950, he was an accomplished coach at the young age of 29. Millikan had worked as the freshman coach and assistant varsity coach for Henry Iba at Oklahoma A & M, and won a national title with the team in 1946. He also was a guard on the Merryville High School team in Missouri that won 53 consecutive games and one state title.

Millikan took over a team that had endured three consecutive losing seasons under coach Flucie Stewart. In Millikan's fourth year as coach, Maryland secured 23 wins and second place in the ACC regular-season standings with a 7-2 record. At the end of that 1953-54 season, Maryland was ranked 20th in the nation after having reached as high as 11 in the national polls. It was the first time the Terps' basketball program received a national top-20 ranking. Three seasons later, Maryland again finished second in the conference during the regular season. The next season, 1957-58, Maryland won its first ACC tournament championship, and Millikan had completed his eighth consecutive season with a winning record.

Despite the team's successes, Millikan wanted out as the Terps' head coach. He was frustrated with what he felt was a low salary compared to his counterparts in the ACC and other conferences, and with a lack of support in recruiting. Millikan says he had only one part-time paid assistant coach to help with recruiting, while other ACC programs had at least two.

After the 1957-58 season, Millikan met with an athletic director at a Big Ten confer-

## BUD MILLIKAN
**Years coached:** 1950-51 to 1966-67
**Record:** 243-182
**Career highlights:**
ACC tournament champion, 1957-58; NCAA East Region third place

ence program during a visit with his parents in Missouri, and was offered the job as head basketball coach.

"I was told the job was mine," he said. "It would have been a better basketball situation. I would have had a full-time assistant coach. I was offered more money (than at Maryland). But, I was told (then-athletic director and head football coach) Jim Tatum would not release me. It was August, right before football practice was about to start. He just didn't want to have to take the time to hire a basketball coach."

Millikan stayed on as head coach and never again matched the success of his first eight years in College Park. The pinnacle of his career was winning the ACC tournament title. The five-year-old ACC conference had established itself as one of the top basketball conferences in the country by the time the 1957-58 season approached. Four conference teams—Duke, North Carolina, North Carolina State and Wake Forest—had each received a top-20 national ranking within the previous three seasons. Maryland was consistently ranked in the top 20 during two of the conference's first five years, reaching as high as number six.

When Millikan took over as head coach, Maryland's nationally recognized football and boxing teams attracted most of the school's athletic attention.

"When Bud came in, he turned the whole program around," said Gene Shue. "Up to that point, Maryland was a football school. Basketball, until Bud got there, was doing nothing. He did a remarkable job. In his first year, it was one of the greatest coaching jobs I've ever seen. He took a ragtag bunch of players and did great with them."

But by 1957, attention afforded the men's basketball team rivaled that of the other two sports. In early February, a home game in the newly built Cole Field House attracted 14,000 fans against top-ranked North Carolina. Maryland lost in double overtime, but the Terps finished second in the conference standings, the third time it had done so in Millikan's brief career.

Maryland's 1957-58 season began with high expectations. Sophomore Al Bunge was a sturdy 6-9 former football player who came along at a time when big men started playing more important roles in a team's success. Forward Charlie McNeil was considered one of the top sophomores in the country. And playmaking guard Tom Young, a senior, returned after some time in the army to co-captain the team. The season also started with some uncertainty. *The Diamondback*, Maryland's school newspaper, reflecting the uncertainty of the starting unit, sponsored a "name the starter" contest. Millikan said his only big concern was sophomore forward Bunge, who lost 55 pounds in the off season due to colitis.

But Bunge rebounded well enough to be ready for the season opener. Four games into the season, the Terps were ranked number six in the country after staying out of the polls the two previous seasons. One of their wins

was over top-ranked Kentucky. About a week after the win, Millikan was quoted in *The Diamondback*, saying, "This is the best team I've ever had, period."

In mid-January, the Terps managed a 13-point win in front of 15,100 Cole Field House fans against number three-ranked and defending national champ North Carolina. *The Diamondback* reported it was the largest crowd to see a basketball game south of New York. Maryland finished the regular season with a 99-59 home win over conference foe South Carolina, and a 9-5 conference record, good enough for fourth place.

The conference tournament featured four teams ranked in the top 17 in the country—Duke, Maryland, N.C. State and North Carolina. The tournament was being held for the fifth time in North Carolina-friendly Reynolds Coliseum in Raleigh, but fourth-seeded Maryland was not intimidated.

"We're not going down there just to keep the railroads in business," said senior point guard Tom Young in the *Baltimore Sun*

Special Collections, University of Maryland Libraries

newspaper. "I know we've got a real good chance, probably the best since the conference began. I do know I'm tired of being eliminated."

In the first-round game against Virginia, the Cavaliers rallied to tie the score at 65. Junior guard Gene Danko then converted a three-point play, and sophomore big man Charlie "Wyatt Earp" McNeil made two free throws with 24 seconds left, and Maryland won 70-66.

Maryland next faced sixth-ranked and top-seeded Duke. The teams split the two-game series during the regular season. In the tournament, Maryland led Duke 53-38 before the Blue Devils stormed back. It took a left-handed hook shot by McNeil at the end of regulation to send the game into overtime. Maryland won in overtime by six points, with McNeil leading the Terps with 22 points and Bunge scoring 11 points and grabbing 14 rebounds. With the win, Maryland was the first team outside of North Carolina to reach the finals of the five-year-old tournament.

In its first conference championship game since the 1938-39 season, the Terps faced 13th-ranked North Carolina. The mostly pro-Carolina fans among the 12,400 at the game helped push the Tar Heels to a 13-point lead late in the first half. "Today, Maryland would go down there and have a mess of fans," said Young. "We had a couple thousand at best."

But Maryland slowly eroded Carolina's lead by scoring 59 points in the second half. The Terps made 40 free throws and won 86-74.

"(North Carolina head coach) Frank McGuire was the kind of coach if he got behind, there were a lot of 'intentional' fouls, instead of stealing the ball to get possession," said Millikan. "I remember we had a very fine night at the free throw line."

After presenting the team trophy to Maryland, Eddie Cameron, chairman of the ACC basketball committee, asked Millikan if he accepted the responsibility of representing the conference in the NCAA tournament. "Yes, Eddie, quite assuredly," Millikan said in *The Diamondback*.

Young still remembers the postgame celebrations, prompted by a rare "no curfew" from Coach Millikan.

"What I remember most is when the game was over," said Young. "We really celebrated. We had some (war) veterans on the team, and wives and girlfriends were down there. And that was a rare thing for Bud Millikan not to have a curfew. The Terrapin Club had a party, we had parties in our rooms, and we partied throughout the town."

Maryland recovered well enough to put on a respectable showing in the school's first ever NCAA tournament appearance. The Terps beat Boston College by 23 points in an East Region first-round game, then lost to Temple in an East Region semifinal by four points. Maryland ended their season with a 59-55 win over Manhattan in East Region consolation game, and a number-six national ranking.

Millikan was never able to again capture the magic of the 1958 ACC title team. Three seniors—Young, Davis and John Nacincik—were the among the team's leading scorers from that team, and Maryland struggled to a losing record the next season.

Four of Millikan's next eight teams suffered losing seasons.

As the Terps struggled throughout the early 1960s, Millikan fell out of favor with some of the Maryland faithful. Students displayed an effigy with the words, "Bud Must Go" in 1963. Some criticized Millikan's preference for plodding play, a slow-down offense supported by a technically sound and aggressive defense.

Dissenters were unhappy with Millikan's inability to recruit top players. Millikan blamed the recruiting woes on insufficient staff, which included one part-time assistant coach.

"Where it hurts you is recruiting," said Millikan. "We had a world of people who came and visited Maryland and liked Maryland, but we didn't get enough early contact with them."

Top prospects generally bypassed Maryland for other ACC schools.

With seven seniors and four juniors on the roster, Maryland managed only a 14-11 season in 1965-66, and lost in the first round of the ACC tournament to North Carolina. The next year, at the end of an 11-14 season, Millikan announced his resignation following a first-round loss to South Carolina in the ACC tournament.

Former players praised Millikan's brilliance, technical innovations in basketball and his priority on academics. He worked his players hard, and many appreciated that.

"Everything we did was difficult," said Shue, an All-American in 1953 and 1954. "On occasion, we would practice three times a day, about two hours each session. You had to do things exactly right. If things weren't going well, we would start running the steps in Ritchie Coliseum. He had drill after drill teaching fundamentals."

When asked if he resigned or was asked to leave, Millikan said it was "50-50. I had been bellyaching for some time to get an assistant. After three or four years of trying, it was hard to be a part of it. I had good times and bad times there."

After leaving Maryland, Millikan moved to near Atlanta and opened an office for a company owned by A.V. Williams, one of the founders of the Terrapin Club. He still lives there today.

When asked if he looks back at his Maryland years fondly, he says, quickly, "Nope, it was just a part of things."

Millikan cherishes a memory in 1966, when Maryland was playing in the Charlotte Invitational. Maryland was 4-3, without its top scorer, Jay McMillen, who was out with injury, and faced Davidson in the tournament opener.

"The host team always picked what they think is the poorest team in the first round," said Millikan.

Maryland beat Davidson, coached by Lefty Driesell, by one point and beat Army, coached by Bobby Knight, by three points to win the tournament.

"I'm probably the only coach in the country who never lost to Lefty and Bobby Knight," said Millikan.

After leaving Maryland following 17 years as head coach, Millikan never coached basketball again.

Maryland Athletics, Media Relations

# BILLY
# JONES

# LEFTY DRIESELL

# TOM
# McMILLEN

The highly anticipated Maryland basketball career of Tom McMillen featured many compelling and dramatic moments. In each of McMillen's three varsity seasons, Maryland endured losses in the finals of the ACC tournament. Two were to N.C. State, including the 103-100 overtime thriller in 1974, which many claim is one of the most exciting college basketball games ever played. In two of those losses, Maryland narrowly missed out on elusive NCAA tournament bids given to the tournament champion. They advanced despite the loss in 1973 because N.C. State was on probation and could not play in the NCAA tournament. That year, Maryland reached the elite eight, marking the furthest NCAA tournament advancement in the program's history.

At the beginning of each of McMillen's three varsity seasons, the preseason national ranking of Maryland's teams was no lower than six. On December 1, 1973, in the Terps' first game of the season, fourth-ranked Maryland lost by one point to number-one ranked UCLA at Pauley Pavilion.

## "It was a dream, just the way I wanted my last game to be."

[TOM McMILLEN]

But none of those moments titillate McMillen's sentimental memories as much as his last home game in Cole Field House as a senior. In that game, on March 2, 1974, the fifth-ranked Terps beat unranked Virginia by 35 points.

## TOM McMILLEN

**Years lettered:** 1971-72, 1972-73, 1973-74
**Position:** Forward
**Season-by-season scoring average:**
    1971-72: 20.8
    1972-73: 21.2
    1973-74: 19.4
**Career highlights:**
    All-America 1972, 1973, 1974; Academic All-America 1972, 1973, 1974; All-ACC 1st team, 1971-72, 1972-73; All-ACC tournament first team 1972, 1973, 1974; All-time leader in career scoring average; Member of 1972 U.S. Olympic team that won a silver medal

Maryland governor Marvin Mandel honored the seniors before the game. After the game, fans from the capacity crowd of 14,500 in Cole field House lifted McMillen and fellow All-America senior Len Elmore on their shoulders and paraded them around the floor. The ceremony culminated in the two cutting down the nets.

"It was a dream, just the way I wanted my last game to be," said McMillen in the school newspaper, *The Diamondback*, after the game. "We went into the game with a businesslike approach. I wasn't overly emotional before the game. I appreciated the quickness of the (pregame) ceremonies. But I got pretty excited during the game."

McMillen also said later he had the "same feeling inside for this one as I did for my first game as a sophomore."

By the time McMillen began his sophomore season, he had received more attention than any other Maryland player before they dribbled their first ball for the varsity. He had been on the cover of national magazines, including *Sports Illustrated* as a high school senior in Mansfield, Pennsylvania. His high school uniform was retired in the Basketball Hall of Fame, for good reason. He averaged 47.7 points and 22.2 rebounds per game.

McMillen picked Maryland after initially committing to North Carolina, in part to stay closer to his hometown. His father, who died when McMillen was a senior, was ill. Also, McMillen's father liked head coach Lefty Driesell, calling him "a man's man." Lefty was also a good salesman.

"He said the president of the United States would be watching the games," said McMillen.

Further, McMillen's brother, Jay, was a top player for the Terps in the mid-1960s. And McMillen felt Maryland was a good investment.

"If you're buying stock, you want to buy it when it's low, not high," he said recently. "Maryland was an undervalued situation. You can go in and help it and get credit for it."

McMillen continued his court dominance on the Terps' freshman team. He scored 48 points in one game and set single-game records for field goals and rebounds. The team won all 16 consecutive games despite losing Elmore to injury for most of season.

McMillen averaged 20.8 points a game as a sophomore, second best in the program's history behind Joe Smith, on a team that finished 27-5, won the National Invitation Tournament and finished the season ranked 14th in the country. That was Maryland's best postseason ranking since the 1957-58 season, when the Terps won the ACC tournament and finished with a number-six ranking.

Maryland did not lose at Cole Field House during the 1971-72 season. The biggest win came against North Carolina in mid-February, the second game between the two teams that season. McMillen called the first game between the two that year in Chapel Hill, "not one of my greatest experiences." The Tar Heels fans considered McMillen a traitor for choosing Maryland over North Carolina. Their jeering prompted head coach

Maryland Athletics, Media Relations

# LEN
# ELMORE

Maryland basketball legend Len Elmore was a New York City-bred, street-wise junior at Maryland when he got to know Terps newcomer John Lucas. Elmore, a native of Queens, New York, found the charismatic Lucas style entertaining.

"Lucas came in as a freshman, and you think, 'Where does this kid come off doing this?' You would laugh at him. He would wear turtlenecks, and a leather coat, and emulate (actor) John Shaft. He wanted to be Shaft, but he had never been to New York City. He was a populist kind of guy."

Elmore remembers when Lucas, who had been at Maryland a short time, drove around a traffic circle on campus in a Dodge Roadrunner for attention to "show how cool his car was," said Elmore, who was sitting in the car at the time. "Then a policeman stops us. He says, 'Mr. Elmore, will you tell this young man we don't do this on this campus?' It was an example of fresh exuberance."

That fresh exuberance was trademark Lucas, and it helped make Lucas arguably the most dynamic basketball player in Maryland history.

"He had great confidence, was outgoing, got along with people," said Driesell. "People just liked him. He was very confident. I loved John Lucas, he was a great leader for me. He was maybe the best leader I've ever had. "

The first time Driesell saw Lucas play was during Driesell's summer camps on the College Park campus after Lucas had graduated from high school. Lucas often played pick-up games in Cole Field House while he attended summer school at Maryland. The first time Driesell saw Lucas play in a formal

competition, Lucas scored 41 points in a North Carolina high school all-star game later that same summer. Driesell also told Lucas he could be a part of the starting unit as a freshman.

Lucas, a high school All-American from Durham, North Carolina, picked Maryland over more than 400 schools. He averaged 34 points per game as a senior at Hillside and once scored 57 points in a game, breaking the league scoring record of the legendary Pete Maravich, one of the most prolific scorers in the history of basketball.

## "Lefty was the deciding factor for me. He was trying to build the 'UCLA of the East.'"

[JOHN LUCAS]

Lucas picked Maryland over such schools as UCLA, which didn't want Lucas to play tennis in college. Coach Driesell allowed Lucas to play tennis, but only after the basketball season ended.

"Lefty was the deciding factor for me," said Lucas. "He was trying to build the 'UCLA of the East'. Duke wasn't good enough, North Carolina State had Monte Towe and Mo Rivers, and North Carolina said they would not let freshman play. Maryland gave me an opportunity."

Lucas said other factors persuaded him to attend Maryland. A sister, who is six years older than Lucas, lived in nearby Silver Spring, Maryland and tennis agent and friend Donald Dell, who represented Arthur Ashe, worked and lived nearby.

Lucas ended his basketball career in College Park as a three-time All-American, joining Tom McMillen as the only Terps to achieve the annual honor three times. He is one of two Maryland players to earn All-ACC first-team honors three times (the other is Juan Dixon). Lucas ranks fifth on the Terps' all-time scoring list (2015) and fourth on the Terps all-time assists list (514), and is in the top five among Maryland freshmen and sophomores in points, assists and scoring average.

A change in a rule by the National Collegiate Athletic Association that prevented freshman from playing varsity sports aided Lucas's prompt elevation to the top of those categories. Lucas

was the first player in Maryland history to play varsity basketball as a freshman and he made an immediate impact on the team. Senior guard Howard White was recovering from a knee injury at the beginning of Lucas's freshman year in 1972, allowing Lucas to join the starting unit in number three-ranked Maryland's season opener on November 29 against Brown University at Cole Field House.

Special Collections, University of Maryland Libraries

In the game, Lucas missed his first shot then made his final nine field goals and finished with 19 points. He added nine assists in the 127-82 Terps win, which set a school record for most points in a game and margin of victory. The following editorial comments in the school newspaper, *The Diamondback*, in the two days following the win proclaimed the positives emanating from the game.

"Four more years. It is not a political proclamation but the length of time the Terps are assured of a top-flight point man. Once the question mark of the squad, the point position has been transformed into a positive point. While everyone was holding their breath with anticipation, freshman John Lucas's performance created an audible sigh of relief from the standing-room-only crowd. The game might have silenced the last of the skeptics over a freshman's ability to compete in varsity play."

Lucas remembers that game as the most profound moment of his career.

"One thing I remember is that I would get beat defensively down the middle, and then Lenny Elmore blocked a guy's shot," said Lucas. "I couldn't believe that. When I played in North Carolina, I didn't have anybody that big. I knew my defense wasn't going to be a factor with Lenny and Owen Brown in the middle. I wasn't expected to do much. I was kind of under the radar."

There were many other luminary moments in Lucas's career. During his final three years at Maryland, Lucas played on teams that were ranked no lower than number 10 in the country and as high as number two.

The Terps advanced to the Elite Eight of the NCAA Tournament during Lucas's freshman and junior seasons.

The Terps' rivalry against N.C. State during Lucas's first two years was easily the most compelling in the country. During his freshman year, Maryland lost to N.C. State twice by two points and a third time by 11 points. One loss was in the first round of the ACC tournament, when State was ranked second in the country. During his sophomore season, N.C. State swept Maryland again, most prominently in the final of the ACC tournament.

Lucas said there were several factors why the Maryland N.C. State rivalry was so strong.

"They had a big center, we had Len Elmore," said Lucas. "It was just good, unbelievable basketball. And teams in North Carolina had a lot of good players—Bobby Jones, Mitch Kupchak, Walter Davis, George Karl. And David Thompson, he would just kill us. State were the kings of Tobacco Road."

Maryland, however, won both regular-season games against the Wolfpack during Lucas's junior and senior seasons.

Lucas was primed for a breakout season in his junior year. He was voted the Most Valuable Player in the International Cup Games in Mexico City, a preseason tournament. But he suffered a broken collarbone in the Terps' opening regular-season game, forcing him out for several games.

Lucas returned to the Maryland lineup six games later and, playing forward at times at six foot four, helped the Terps win the ACC regular-season championship. One noteworthy game was at Duke in early February. Lucas scored 25 points in Maryland's 104-80 route in his hometown of Durham, despite some heckling from the fans. During game introductions, a fan threw a tennis ball at Lucas. Lucas joked after the game that he thought a member of the media threw the ball. The Terps' 104 points that night were the most ever scored against Duke at Cameron Indoor Stadium. But the season ended abruptly for Maryland. The second-ranked Terps lost to eighth-ranked N.C. State by two points in a semifinal game of the ACC tournament.

Maryland lost two senior starters from the 1974-75 team, and enjoyed a number-three preseason ranking for the second time in Lucas's career. Maryland took an 11-0 record and a number-two national ranking into its first ACC game against seventh-ranked Wake Forest. Lucas scored a career-high 34 points, but the Terps lost by three points. Maryland, plagued by injury and academic probations, never reached its full potential that season. One of four ACC teams ranked in the nation's top ten at some point during the season, Maryland finished in a second-place tie in the conference with a 7-5 record. Maryland lost in the semifinals of the ACC tournament to unranked Virginia and did not receive a bid to the NCAA tournament.

As a tennis player, Lucas went undefeated in high school and played on a Junior Davis Cup team. He was an ACC doubles champion his freshman year and twice was the ACC singles champion.

Maryland fans remember Lucas as much for his personality as his athletic skills. He shined in the spotlight and flourished in solitude. He has said he felt at ease and happiest when alone, and that the best thing is being puzzling to people. He said he wanted to be both a bum and president of the United States.

"My message was, you don't know what things that God has in store for you, or the experiences you [will] go through," he said. "I was going to have to go out and find my wisdom. My family gave me that insight."

Lucas was the number-one pick in the NBA draft in 1976 and played 14 years in the league. He later coached six years in the NBA and was a league general manager for two years. While playing in the NBA, Lucas became addicted to drugs. Following his playing days, Lucas started the Houston, Texas, based John Lucas Enterprises, which runs a number of drug-treatment programs and other endeavors that help athletes, and others, maintain their sobriety and work to improve their quality of life.

"You don't know what things that God has in store for you, or the experiences you [will] go through."

[JOHN LUCAS]

# BRAD
# DAVIS

# TARA
# HEISS

Tara Heiss showed early in her Terps career why she was destined to be a Maryland basketball legend. During her freshman season, in 1974-75, Heiss made her first varsity appearance during a game against Frostburg State, five games into the season. Heiss entered the game with 12 minutes to go, the last of Maryland's 13 players to see action. Heiss made all seven of her shots, plus two throws, to lead the team with 16 points in a 102-31 romp. In the regular-season finale against Federal City College, Maryland went on a 23-8 run after Heiss entered the game, and took a 25-24 lead, after having fallen behind 16-2. Heiss shared the team lead in scoring with 14 points in a 12-point loss.

Heiss broke into the starting lineup when 7-5 Maryland began the state tournament. Maryland won all three games in the tournament by at least 16 points, and Heiss scored 22 points in the tournament final.

# "She's probably one of the best players I've ever seen, among all players and all programs."

[COACH CHRIS WELLER]

During her sophomore year, Heiss became such a prolific offensive player she was compared to Brad Davis and John Lucas on Maryland's men's team. On the way to averaging 16.2 points a game for the season, Heiss drew this praise from *The Diamondback* newspaper columnist Vincent Paterno in January, 1976. "There are those who claim the growth of women's basketball is being held back because there are few players with the crowd pleasing potential found in the men's game. If any woman cager at the University is to rectify this, it will be sophomore guard Tara Heiss. She is nearly as much a joy to watch in action as any of Lefty Driesell's three backcourt men."

When asked during her career if she patterned her game after the dynamic Davis, she replied, "No, he doesn't shoot very well." She then smiled and said she was joking. Chris Weller, Maryland's head coach for three of Heiss's four seasons at Maryland, commented in 2002 in *The Diamondback* on Heiss's playing ability as well as her sense of humor.

"She's probably one of the best players I've ever seen, among all players and all programs," said Weller. "She was quick, skilled and she was a player's player. People loved to play with Tara because she never took anything that seriously. She always just loved the game. I remember we'd be playing anoth-

---

## TARA HEISS

**Years lettered:** 1974-75, 1975-76, 1976-77, 1977-78

**Position:** Guard

**Season-by-season scoring average:**
- 1974-75: 10.8
- 1975-76: 16.2
- 1976-77: 14.7
- 1977-78: 14.3

**Career highlights:**
All-Region 1978; U.S. Olympic Team 1980; U.S. Pan American Team 1979; ACC tournament MVP 1978; All-ACC tournament team, 1978

er team and they'd make a great play and she'd say, 'Great play,' and I'd say, 'Tara, we're competing against them.' She'd just say, 'But, you got to admit, it was a great play.'"

More often, Heiss was the one creating the great plays. During her sophomore season, Heiss scored 34 points in a win over Delaware that broke the Maryland single-game scoring record of 30 points, set three days earlier by Mary Briese. She stands fourth on the all-time single-game scoring list. As a junior and senior, Heiss increased her focus on assists. She holds Maryland's single-season assists record set during her senior year. Further, she ranks second on the Terps' all-time assists list.

Much was expected of Maryland's team during Heiss's senior season in 1977-78. Earlier that year, Weller said the Terps had enough talent to be the top team in the country. The team's top three scorers were Heiss and two freshman, Kris Kirchner and Betsy Bailey.

But Heiss was clearly the team's main threat. She was the first Maryland women's basketball player to score 1,000 points, doing so

in the number-eight-ranked and unbeaten Terps win over number-14 Penn State in January, 1978. She set a team record with 14

Special Collections, University of Maryland Libraries

# ALBERT KING

I owned one of the best perspectives in the sold-out, frenzied arena. As center Larry Gibson stood at the free throw line, preparing an attempt to complete a three-point play with one second remaining in a game against number—one ranked Notre Dame, I stood about 15 feet behind the basket, in a clearance between two floor-seat sections of Cole Field House. It was one of the benefits of being a student usher at basketball games at the arena. An impressionable junior, I had a glorious, uncluttered view of history about to be made on that late January evening in 1979.

Gibson converted the free throw to beat the number-one ranked Irish, and seconds later, fans rushed the court. One of my jobs was to keep the court clear of spectators after games. One-hundred-fifty pounds was not a formidable force against a crazed crowd. I didn't attempt to thwart the throng.

## "I used to dream about being a star and playing basketball."

[ALBERT KING]

Albert King had even a better view of Maryland's one-point victory. Moments earlier, King had set a pick that set Greg Manning free for an open shot in the corner. Manning opted instead to drive to the basket, looking for an opening to shoot the potential game-tying basket. As he was nearly falling out of bounds, he tossed the ball to Gibson, who made a lay-up and got fouled.

## ALBERT KING

**Years lettered:** 1977-78, 1978-79, 1979-80, 1980-81
**Position:** Forward
**Season-by-season scoring average:**
　　1977-78: 13.8
　　1978-79: 15.9
　　1979-80: 21.7
　　1980-81: 18.0
**Career highlights:**
　　All-America 1980, 1981; ACC Player of the Year, 1980; All-ACC selection 1980, 1981; All-ACC tournament selection 1980, 1981; Number 3 all-time Maryland scorer

After Notre Dame called two time outs, Gibson walked to the free throw line and King walked to the other end of the court, and stood under Maryland's basket. Before he shot, Gibson called out to King, "I've got it." King nodded and crossed all his fingers for good luck. Gibson made the free throw, and bedlam reigned.

Of the eight times in the program's history Maryland has beaten a top-ranked opponent, no game was determined by a closer margin. King did not achieve milestone numbers in the game—eight points, four assists and four rebounds—but for King, it was the most memorable reflection on a much-anticipated career that some consider fell short of expectations.

The expectations and excitement created by the thought of King attending Maryland was compared to that of three-time All-American Tom McMillen and Moses Malone, who agreed to play for Maryland but changed his mind and opted for a professional career instead. King averaged 38.6 points and 22 rebounds per game his senior year at Fort Hamilton High in Brooklyn, New York and was considered the top high school recruit in the country. He was featured in *Sports Illustrated* magazine at the age of 15, and was, as *The Diamondback* newspaper put it, "considered among the best basketball players ever produced by New York city's fertile playgrounds." His older brother, Bernard, had been a star at the University of Tennessee and began a prominent NBA career the year Albert joined Maryland. King's yearnings to thrive at basketball began at an early age while playing ball on the mean streets of Brooklyn.

"I used to dream about being a star and playing basketball," he said in *The Diamondback* during his junior season. "A lot of guys wanted to be pimps, because I guess they looked up to people that made money. I was really a quiet person, and basketball was a way to get away from all the violence. I think the big thing that kept me from hanging out on the streets, drinking and smoking and doing all that was my parents. I was scared what my mother and father would do to me. There were always certain rules you had to follow. They used to always make me be home and I hated that. I'd have to lie, say I didn't feel good, but everyone knew my mother wanted me home."

King picked Maryland over Arizona State because he said that the school provided a better chance of playing pro ball.

"It had more to offer in terms of coaching, ability of its players and its national rankings," he said while at Maryland.

Despite averaging in double figures his freshman and sophomore seasons, many felt King did not live up to the hype during those two years. It did not help King that Maryland finished 15-13 during his freshman year, and did not play in a postseason tournament.

King was quoted in the *Washington Post* before his sophomore season began, saying, "I guess I didn't know what bad was until last year." King endured bouts of tonsillitis and mononucleosis and lost weight before his freshman season began. During games, he admitted to checking his halftime statistics to see if he had reached scored his average.

King said in *The Diamondback* that he felt the pressure of the hype his first two years.

Maryland Athletics, Media Relations

"I used to ask myself, 'Am I really a good ballplayer?' I knew I wasn't living up to the standards of others. I lost some confidence in my ability as a player. People were real nice to me, though. They'd always congratulate me after games even though I knew in the back of their minds that they didn't think I was playing up to my capabilities."

The next season, Maryland finished 19-11 and lost in the second round of the NIT. King had much to do with the team's improvement and started showing signs of his greatness late in his sophomore season. He scored a then-career-high 30 points in a loss at Virginia. He led the Terps past Clemson in the first round of the ACC tournament with a team-high 20 points, including the eventual game-winner. In the first round of the NIT, King converted both ends of a one-and-one with three seconds remaining in a triple-overtime win over Rhode Island at Cole Field House. He missed the first 27 minutes of the game with an injured foot but finished with 15 points. King entered the game with 13:09 remaining in the second half and the Terps trailing 39-34 and then scored nine points the rest of the half. In the next game, he scored 27 points in a loss to Ohio State.

King's fortunes improved during his junior season. He was the leading scorer (21.7 points per game) on a team that won the ACC regular-season title. King scored 32 points in a win over Wake Forest that clinched the regular season championship. His 38 points in Maryland's six-point win over Clemson in the first round of the ACC tournament ties a Maryland record in the tournament along with Walt Williams. King was voted ACC

Player of the Year and was a first-team All-American.

Maryland that year lost in the ACC tournament final by one point to Duke and advanced to the NCAA Tournament Sweet Sixteen, where Maryland lost in a dramatic and disappointing game to Georgetown.

In the loss to Duke, King's last-second jump shot bounced around the rim before falling away, leaving him in tears in the locker room after the game. As he sat in his chair sobbing, Coach Lefty Driesell walked over to King to console him.

"I should have made it, Coach," said King. "I'm sorry, I'm sorry I missed it."

King said during his senior season that his breakout junior season was the result of being more comfortable with life in general.

"I think your personality on the court changes with your personality off the court. I started feeling more comfortable with my surroundings here at the university, and it was reflected in the way I played basketball."

Maryland received a number-four preseason ranking during King's senior season, the team's highest preseason ranking since 1975. Early in the season, Coach Lefty Driesell said for the Terps to be great, King had to be great. It appeared he was not. In Maryland's nine losses that season, King averaged 14.7 points and scored 20 points only once. The Terps slowly fell in the rankings as the season progressed. By the time Maryland hosted number-five Wake Forest in the last home game of the season, the Terps had fallen to number 20 in the national poll. In its previous game, Maryland played an uninspired game and lost at home to number-10 ranked North Carolina by 13 points. The next day, King uncharacteristically criticized Maryland fans for booing the Terps during the loss.

## "I started feeling more comfortable with my surroundings here at the university, and it was reflected in the way I played basketball."

[ALBERT KING]

"I don't think something like that would happen in any other gym in the ACC," he said at the time. "When we're on the road, okay, I expect to get booed."

King and Maryland rebounded against Wake Forest on Senior Night. He scored 28 points, making 13 of 16 field goals in Maryland's 14-point win. King took the game over with Maryland up by six points and with ten minutes remaining. In the next four minutes, he made six of six shots, had two assists, one steal and one rebound. Inspired by Maryland's 19-point lead, the Cole Field House fans starting chanting "Albert!" King said after the game that the presence of his parents, who he had not seen since the previous summer, helped inspire his performance.

Some two weeks later, Maryland upset number-four ranked Virginia by three points in a semifinal game of the ACC tournament behind King's 24 points. But he scored only 10 points in the Terps' one-point loss to number-12 ranked North Carolina in the tournament final.

King stormed back with a commanding 25-point performance in a 12-point win over Tennessee-Chattanooga in the first round of the NCAA Tournament. He scored 22 points against Indiana in the tournament's second-round game, but he shot 10 of 28 from the field in the 35-point loss to the Hoosiers. It was a symbolic ending to King's Maryland career—a pretty good performance that just wasn't good enough.

During his senior year, King surpassed John Lucas as Maryland's all-time leading scorer (he now ranks third) and was named All-American and All-ACC for the second consecutive year.

King never welcomed the spotlight that seemed to shine too brightly throughout his Maryland career.

"People would say, 'Albert doesn't like basketball, he doesn't like to talk about basketball,'" he said in *The Diamondback*. "It's not that I don't like to talk about it, it's not that I hate it. I love it, it's benefiting me and my family; it's just that I don't like the stereotype of the jock."

King played in the NBA for nine seasons, and works as a restaurant manager in Brooklyn.

# ADRIAN BRANCH

It was an environment where a true Maryland basketball legend could shine. Hundreds of Maryland basketball faithful gathered to rally their team to an unlikely championship run at the 2004 ACC Men's Basketball Tournament in Greensboro, North Carolina. They walked around a Terrapin flea market of tables set up in a rectangular formation in a hallway of the team hotel. They buzzed with enthusiasm and excitement, snatching up all types of Maryland memorabilia and clothing. Members of the Maryland alumni association could barely keep pace processing the plethora of purchases.

Most of the throng at some point crammed into the adjacent grand ballroom to hear a spirited speech from head coach Gary Williams, and to meet some of the Terps players. Later, as the size of the group began to dissipate, former Terp scoring machine Adrian Branch walked casually toward the tables, igniting pockets of energy as fans recognized the Terps hoops legend.

Unknown to most at the alumni event, Branch would be honored as an ACC basketball legend during a dinner two nights later. He shook hands, slapped shoulders, and hugged acquaintances. His positive aura and marquee smile permeated the room. It was as if Branch revived the faded spirits of the ACC basketball tournament champion Terps. Branch was a member of the last Maryland team to win an ACC tournament, in 1984.

A few minutes after making his comfortably grand entrance, Branch walked over to where I was sitting in an unused cloakroom next to the hall, where I was signing copies of my first Terps book, *Tales from the Maryland*

*Terrapins*, an anecdotal history of Terps athletics. I had met Branch in the early 1990s at a celebrity basketball game that benefited a group that supported physically disabled athletes. We had developed a distant, but comfortable friendship. He talked eloquently about his days at Maryland for my books on Maryland athletics.

Armed in part with an NBA championship ring from his time playing with the Los Angeles Lakers, Branch has become a prominent motivational speaker, espousing the importance of setting goals, especially to young people. True to form, he quickly ingrained an uplifting message into our conversation.

"It was 20 years ago when we won our last ACC tournament," he said, with his trademark broad, engaging grin. "We did it right here in Greensboro, at the same Coliseum they're playing in this weekend. I feel it. I think we're gonna win it again."

Perhaps moved by Branch's wishful message, the basketball spirits helped propel the Terps to the tournament title three days later. Branch sat about a half-dozen rows behind the Maryland bench throughout the entire tournament, watching an ACC tournament for the first time as a spectator since leading Maryland to the 1984 title.

"I saw one from a fan's perspective," said Branch. "You could sit and enjoy the popcorn, the atmosphere. It was a new experience for me being in the red and white, living and hanging on every possession. When you play, the tournament happens so fast, you get to feel a little of the crowd, but then you're gone. As a player, you don't walk through the crowd. Believe it or not, everyone comes to see you, but you might be some of the most isolated people in the whole place.

"I remember in the championship game, Duke made its traditional run. I remember just saying a silent prayer, 'It would be nice to one time flip the switch on Duke.' That was a thrill. I was happy for Maryland, I was happy for the past, present and future of Maryland."

Branch had a profound effect on Maryland's past during the 1984 ACC tournament. A junior, Branch scored 12 points in the 14th-ranked Terps' first-round, six-point win over defending national champion N.C. State. Maryland led throughout most of the game and were ahead by just one point about midway through the half when Branch took a rebound after a missed N.C. State shot, drove the length of the floor and was fouled while converting a layup. That put the Terps up 49-45. Branch's 12 points were just below his 13.0 per-game season average.

In a semifinal game against Wake Forest, Maryland bolted to a 33-20 lead at halftime. Wake Forest fought back to within three points before Branch then helped the Terps break the game open. Twice, the six-foot-

eight Branch took six-foot-two Wake guard Delany Rudd one on one and converted jumpers. Branch led the Terps in scoring with 16 points along with center Ben Coleman, and Maryland won the game by two points. The Terps received a break when Duke beat number one-ranked North Carolina by two points in the other semifinal game.

## "I remember just saying a silent prayer, 'It would be nice to one time flip the switch on Duke.'"

[ADRIAN BRANCH]

The previous time Maryland and Duke played in an ACC final in 1980, Albert King's shot at the buzzer bounced off the rim twice, allowing the Blue Devils to escape with a one-point win. The 1984 final was destined to be just as close. The Terps and 16th-ranked Duke had split two games during the regular season. Maryland won the first game by six, and Duke won the second contest by five. The Duke loss was Branch's first game back after serving a suspension for being convicted of marijuana possession.

Branch uses that experience to teach youth today to stay away from drugs. "It's not where you've been, it's where you're going," said Branch. "It's how you finish. You want to know if you're mixed up or fixed up."

Maryland fell behind early to Duke in the 1984 championship game, and trailed by three at halftime. Branch shot three of eight from the field and Len Bias had committed six turnovers. Branch recounted Coach Lefty Driesell's halftime speech in *The Diamondback* the day after the game. "[Driesell] told us at halftime that even though we played badly, we were still only three points behind," he said. "He told us if we played like we can, we could win the game."

Duke extended its lead to 42-34 early in the second half, but Branch then converted a short bank shot that sparked a 24-3 Maryland run, and Maryland held on to win 74-62. The following passage in *The Diamondback* captured the jubilant chaos that ensued.

"In the frenzied moments following the final horn, the coliseum court resembled a jammin' disco dance floor. First Bias and Herman Veal paired off, then Bias did a solo number while Mark Fothergill and Jeff Baxter supplied hand-clap chorus. Then Coleman and Branch did a two-step under the basket. And the band played on—endless renditions of the Amen chorus filled the emptying coliseum as the Terps and their parents and fans danced and sang and shouted and danced some more. But Driesell never got his shot at cutting down a net. By the time he had finished his obligatory television interviews, his ravenous players had already assaulted both ends of the court. (Herman) Veal wore one net, while the other adorned the shoulders of Bias. After the initial hilarity had died down and shower time arrived, the Terps had tried their hand at toting Driesell off the court. It took a combined effort of Coleman, (Mark) Fothergill, Veal and (Jeff) Baxter to lug the guy 10 steps before they wisely set him down."

During Branch's senior year, Maryland lost to Duke in the first

Maryland Athletics, Media Relations

round of the ACC tournament, but Maryland advanced to the NCAA Tournament Sweet 16 for the second consecutive year. The only time Maryland did not play in the NCAA tournament during Branch's four years at Maryland was during his freshman year.

Branch grew up 15 minutes from College Park, in Seat Pleasant, and was an All-American at DeMatha High School, at that time one of the top high school programs in the nation. When Dean Smith visited his house on a recruiting trip, Branch admits his ego was raging.

"Smith was sitting there talking to my parents, getting to know them, and I said to him, 'So when are you gonna give me a recruiting pitch?'" said Branch. "He said, 'Adrian, me knocking on your door means we want you to come to the university.' You never saw a big head shrink so quickly."

Branch picked Maryland primarily because it was close to home. He had tired of all the traveling he had done with AAU teams since he was 12. And with Albert King, Buck Williams, Ernest Graham and Greg Manning leaving the team, Branch figured he would see ample court time soon. And he admits he was a little full of himself. According to the book, *Cole Classics*, when a reporter asked him shortly after committing to Maryland who might start for the Terps the next season, he replied, "Me and four other guys." In that book he said, "I was always confident. You're either the predator or the prey."

Branch said he expected to be a secondary scorer for the Terps his freshman year. "I came in the first day of practice and started passing the ball around," he said in *Cole Classics*. "Lefty, in his southern drawl, said, 'Son, I need you to shoot the ball. I don't need you passing.'"

Branch shot the ball plenty, leading the team in scoring with a 15.2 average. He surpassed John Lucas as the leading scorer for Terps freshman, a record since broken by Joe Smith. Branch is fourth on Maryland's all-time scoring list with 2,017 points.

One of the more dramatic moments in Branch's career came during his freshman year. Branch hit the game-winning shot against number-one ranked Virginia in the last regular-season game of the season. The 15-footer from the foul line fell through the basket as time expired. Branch scored 29 points, making 12 of 17 shots from the field. After the game, coach Lefty Driesell said Branch joined Lucas as the best freshmen he ever coached.

Branch led the ACC in scoring for freshman, bettering Michael Jordan's 13.5 points per game. But Jordan, part of a national championship team that year at Carolina, beat him out in the conference Freshman of the Year voting.

"What Michael meant to his team and what I meant to my team was totally different. He was just tagging along."

Now, Branch still stands by that statement.

"I brought the noise," he said. "I was privileged to be our guy. Mike had on his team the number-one pick in the (1982 NBA) draft, James Worthy, and Sam Perkins, the number-four pick in the (1984) draft. He could make mistakes and be protected. I had to go for what I knew."

# BUCK
# WILLIAMS

consistently been great against us. One is Buck Williams. The other is Ralph Sampson." Teammate Greg Manning, said, "Sometimes I look at him and I'm just thankful he's on my side. On that court he's just as glad to tear your head off as shake your hand."

The *Post* article reported that when Duke played Maryland at Cole Field House in 1981, Williams growled at Duke center Mike Tissaw when they shook hands before the game.

"When I put on those sneakers, I can't let anybody get in my way," Williams said in the article. "There are too many things I have to do, too many goals I haven't reached yet. Ever since I've been a kid, I've had one goal in life...to buy my mother a house. I know the way for me to reach that goal is through basketball, and I'm determined not to let anything stop me from doing it."

Williams did not let a broken finger that forced him to miss seven games early in his sophomore season stop him from having a productive year. He helped Maryland advance to the NCAA tournament for the first time since 1975. Williams's rebounding average (10.1) dropped a bit that year, but he raised his scoring average by nearly six points, to 15.5. Only sharp-shooting guard Manning had a better field goal percentage than Williams. Also, Maryland ended the season with a number-eight national ranking.

With Williams joining returning starters King, Manning, Graham and Reggie Jackson, Maryland received a number-four preseason ranking for the 1980-81 season. After losing to unranked Louisville in mid-December, ninth-ranked Maryland rebounded in its next game with an overtime win against N.C. State, in a game that marked the conference coaching debut of Valvano. Williams converted a three-point play at the end of regulation to tie the game.

Williams proved he could score points in tough situations. In late January 1981, he scored six of Maryland's seven points during overtime, making all four of his foul shots, in a 69-66 win over Pitt. In a three-point loss to 13th-ranked Notre Dame, Williams scored 20 points and grabbed 11 rebounds while battling the flu.

Williams was a member of the 1980 U.S. Olympic basketball team, but did not compete in the Summer Olympics because the U.S. boycotted those games. He decided to enter the NBA draft following his junior season after the Detroit Pistons and the New Jersey Nets guaranteed they would make him their top draft pick. The Nets took Williams as the third pick in the draft, and Williams played 18 years in the NBA, the longest of any former Terp player, with the Nets, the Portland Trail Blazers and the New York Knicks.

# LEN
# BIAS

emories of Len Bias at Maryland prompt conflicting themes: momentous triumphs and monumental tragedy; magical athleticism and mysterious behavior; magnanimous dunks and mystical death. No other Maryland basketball player has captured the attention of basketball fans with the same compelling combination of elation and sorrow. Len Bias brought Maryland basketball to dizzying heights and drowning lows. His days at Maryland showed us only what could have been, and should have been—potentially one of the greatest basketball players of a generation. With Len Bias, would there have been the same Michael Jordan?

Bias made a strong impact on his team in both his freshman and sophomore seasons. Bias started 13 of 30 games his freshman season, and was the fourth leading scorer that year with a 7.1 points per game on a team that advanced to the second round of the ACC tournament.

Bias blossomed his sophomore year, punctuated by his performance in the ACC tournament championship win over Duke in 1984. Admittedly motivated by not being named to the All-ACC team that season, Bias scored 26 points on 12-of-17 shooting from the field. He dunked to open the second half, cutting Duke's lead to one point, and then scored 10 of Maryland's points in a 24-3 run that helped clinch the Terps' first ACC tournament title since 1958. Bias ended that season as the Terps' second-leading scorer (15.2), one-tenth of a point behind Ben Coleman.

As a junior, Bias led Maryland in scoring (18.9 points) and rebounding (6.8) and became the sixth Terp in history to be named

an All-American as a junior. He was also the first Maryland player named ACC Player of the Year as a junior, and the only one who received that honor twice.

Bias was one of only two seniors on the team in 1985-86, and the Terps' lack of experience showed. Maryland was ranked 17th when it lost to an unranked Ohio State team in the third game of the season, and failed to achieve a national ranking the remainder of the year. Maryland lost eight of 10 games in the middle of the season, including its first six ACC games, before beating Clemson and N.C. State.

Bias, along with guards Jeff Baxter and John Johnson, squashed that momentum by missing curfew after the N.C. State game. They were suspended for the next game against Clemson, which Maryland lost by 10 points, leaving them at 13-11 overall and 3-7 in the conference.

An NCAA bid seemed tenuous at best. After a 47-point romp over lowly University of Maryland-Eastern Shore, Maryland resumed ACC play against number-one ranked and once-beaten North Carolina in Chapel Hill. Driesell said after the win over UMES that Maryland needed to win three of its last four games to "definitely" get an NCAA bid.

Thanks in large part to Bias's 35 points, Maryland mastered a shocking five-point win over UNC that ranks as one of Maryland's most dramatic wins ever. Maryland was behind by nine points with 2:58 remaining when Bias scored on two successive dunks, the second after stealing Carolina's inbounds pass. Bias then hit a jump shot with 48 seconds to go to pull Maryland within two, and Baxter hit a 20-footer with two seconds left to send the game into overtime.

Bias even played a small part in Baxter's winning shot. Baxter would not have had a chance to tie the game if not for Kenny Smith missing the front end of a one-and-one free throw. Baxter claims Bias told Smith, "Now's the time to choke, Kenny," as he prepared to shoot the free throws.

Bias converted a jumper with 1:51 left that put Maryland ahead for good, 73-72. With Maryland clinging to the one-point lead, Bias then blocked Kenny Smith's shot in the lane with 10 seconds remaining to clinch the win. Keith Gatlin scored Maryland's final four points, two after throwing Maryland's inbounds pass off of

Smith's back, then collecting the bouncing ball and converting a lay-up.

Bias's heroics were not confined to late in the game. With Maryland down by 11 points and two minutes remaining in the first half, Bias scored six consecutive points.

After the game, Driesell called Bias's performance the best he had ever seen. Two days after the game, *Washington Post* columnist Thomas Boswell called Bias "The Answer", for his ability to respond when his team is in

Maryland Athletics, Media Relations

# CHRIS WELLER

Chris Weller clearly demonstrated her proficient skill during her first year as head coach of the women's basketball team at Maryland in 1975-76. The Lady Terps won their first eight games and boasted a 12-1 record when they faced national powerhouse Immaculata at Cole Field House in mid-February. Immaculata came to College Park with an 11-1 record and winners of three of the previous four national collegiate championships. They also featured Cathy Rush, one of the top coaches in the country.

Weller was worried about more than beating one of best programs in the nation that day. She also was aware that Rush was being considered to replace her as Maryland's coach. Maryland athletic director Jim Kehoe interviewed Rush for the job earlier in the day

## CHRIS WELLER

**Years coached:** 1975-2002
**Record:** 499-286
**Career highlights:**
AIAW Runner-up, 1978; NCAA tournament: Final Four 1982, 1989; Elite Eight 1988, 1992; Sweet Sixteen 1983, 1990; First round, 1984, 1986, 1991, 1993; 1997, 2001; ACC champions 1978, 1979, 1981, 1982, 1983, 1986, 1988, 1989; Naismith National Coach of the Year 1992; ACC Coach of the Year 1989, 1992

"Some parents went in and spoke on my behalf," said Weller. "I didn't get involved with it. I'm not a political person. But I wanted to be the permanent person. I would get nervous when anyone said (Rush's) name. I really focused more on the team."

Immaculata won the game by one point, but Weller won the battle to keep her job. No players needed to quit, and Weller ultimately achieved a high level of job security. In her 27 years as the team's head coach—the longest tenure of any women's coach at Maryland—Weller won eight ACC tournament championships, the most of any conference team; made 16 NCAA and Association for Intercollegiate Athletics for Women tournament appearances, and advanced to one national championship title game. Weller was the Naismith National Coach of the Year in 1992, the year Maryland made its only appearance atop the national rankings. Also that year, Weller was ACC Coach of the Year for the second time.

> ## "I wanted our players to know nobody was more important than they were. It was one of the smartest moves I ever made as a coach."
>
> [COACH CHRIS WELLER]

of the game. Weller started the season as an interim head coach, and, with her team primed to pull an upset over Immaculata, her job was no more secure than before the Terps' first game of the season. *The Diamondback* newspaper reported that some Maryland players had threatened to quit if Weller was not named as permanent head coach.

The Terps' 16-point loss to UCLA in the 1978 AIAW title game capped Weller's most memorable season as the Terps head coach.

Weller's first team finished 20-4 in 1976, and her second team fared nearly as well, completing the 1977 season at 17-6. For the first time, Weller that season received four scholarships for her team. She allocated two for new recruits and two for current players.

"I wanted our players to know nobody was more important than they were," she said. "It was one of the smartest moves I made as a coach. There was no resentment."

Prior to the start of the 1977-78 season, Weller proclaimed the Terps had enough talent to be the top team in the country. And Weller wanted to showcase her talent against the top teams in the nation, scheduling games against UCLA and Kansas, among others. That season also marked the debut of the women's ACC basketball tournament. Could Maryland pull off a legendary double—ACC tournament title and national championship?

Entering the conference tournament, played then before the end of the regular season, Maryland sported a 13-1 record. Their only loss was to N.C. State, by 12 points. The Terps cruised through the first- and second-round games, and faced the number-two ranked Wolfpack in the final. In that game, Maryland scored the final six points of the first half to open a six-point lead, and never looked back. Guard Tara Heiss ran a dynamic fast break for the Terps, scored a game-high 30 points and was voted the tournament's Most Valuable Player.

But defense won the game for Maryland. Weller blamed poor defense for Maryland's loss earlier in the season to N.C. State. During the two weeks between that loss and the ACC tournament championship, Weller worked hard to teach a new defensive system she called "82", which Maryland debuted at the tournament.

The Terps focused much of their defensive effort on State's All-America center Genia Beasley, who scored 30 points in State's earlier win against Maryland. Weller had freshman Kris Kirchner defend Beasley, who scored 24 points on 11-of-26 shooting. After the game, Wolfpack coach Kay Yow said Beasley was "really forcing her shots...and I don't know why."

Weller initially did not explain the nuances of the defense. She said after the game that the system is "uniquely ours." Recently, Weller explained the defense.

"It was a three-quarter-court zone," said Weller. "We weren't quick enough to go full court, but we didn't want to sit in the quarter court because we had to stretch their offense."

Winning the ACC title did not clinch a national tournament berth for the Terps. They needed to finish either first or second in the Eastern Region of the AIAW tournament to play in the national tournament. Maryland won its last five games of the regular season, including a five-point win over Immaculata during senior night at Cole Field House. As a result of their strong finish, Maryland hosted its first two games in the regional tournament, and won both games. Up next was a rematch against Immaculata at the school's home court in West Chester, Pennsylvania. Maryland won by one point, beating Immaculata for only the second time, after a Macs player missed a last-second lay-up and

Maryland had blown a 15-point lead. Heiss again led the Terps with 31 points.

"It was very tough to win in Philadelphia, in Immaculata's back yard," said Weller. "I was excited we were going to nationals, but I was relieved because I know we could have been upset. I would have considered it an upset. A lot of people thought we weren't ready to play in nationals."

The win clinched Maryland's first national tournament berth despite losing to Montclair State in the Eastern Region title game. But sixth-ranked Maryland first faced top-ranked Tennessee in the 16-team tournament. Maryland shot 61 percent from the field to upset the Volunteers, and then beat Southern Connecticut by 40 points, and Wayland Baptist by five points to reach the tournament final.

But Maryland fell flat in the final against UCLA, which the Terps has beaten earlier in the season. The Bruins were playing on a home court where they had won 32-consecutive games, and came into the game with a 21-game winning streak. They broke open a close game at the end of the first half, led at the break by 10 points and won by 16 points. "I think we just ran into a hornet's nest," Weller said after the game. "They shut down everything we tried."

Still, reaching the national final was quite an accomplishment.

"That was my very first team coaching at Maryland," said Weller. "I grew into the concept of college coaching with them."

Weller compares the success of her 1989 team with the accomplishments of the 1978 squad. Unlike that team, much was expected of the 1989 group that included four of the top six scorers from a team that finished the previous year 26-6, won the ACC tournament for the second time in three years and advanced to the NCAA tournament Elite Eight. The team included two senior All-Americans, Vicky Bullett and Deanna Tate, numbers one and five, respectively in the Terps' all-time leading scoring list.

> ## "That was my very first team coaching at Maryland. I grew into the concept of college coaching with them."
>
> [COACH CHRIS WELLER]

Maryland lost just once during the ACC regular season—by two points to Clemson—and entered the ACC tournament with a 23-2 record. They continued their conference dominance by storming through the tournament, winning the three games by an average of 21 points. Maryland advanced to the NCAA Final Four for the second time in the program's history, losing to Tennessee by eight points.

Weller says that team was special for many reasons.

"It was after Len Bias died, and coaches and players were leaving and transferring," she said. "It was horrible for the athletes. They were constantly in the newspapers because of Bias. There are some groups you grow with. They became very special. We called ourselves 'the survivors.'"

They could also have called themselves the entertainers. During the last road trip of the regular season, some players staged a talent show in the hotel where they stayed.

"They were imitating singers," said Weller. "But I didn't get it. I didn't know who they were. I would say, 'Who's that?' Bullett won hands down for her Stevie Wonder imitation. Subrena Rivers, Christy Winters, Tate and Kaisa Maine imitated a rap group."

The team possessed a special level of camaraderie. Bullett placed inspirational thoughts on her teammates' lockers.

Weller's Maryland athletic career began in 1962, when she first played on the women's basketball team she said was called an "interest group". They practiced and played their home games at Prinkert Field House, which allowed for a standing-room crowd of only 25 people.

"We had a real home-court advantage," said Weller. "We knew where the bad spots were. At one end, you would slide into the wall. At the other end, there were splinters in the floor. And there was no concept of training."

Weller also was a member of the women's lacrosse and swimming "interest groups" at Maryland. "We took care of the field ourselves," said Weller. "If it had holes, we'd bring dirt and plant some seeds and water it. It sounds a little bizarre. What was wrong with us? We were college kids. We got a coach ourselves, and ran the schedule ourselves. It was fun."

Weller transferred that competitiveness to the bench when she became an assistant coach for Dottie McKnight for the 1973-74 season for a $300 graduate assistant stipend. When she accepted the head coaching position, Weller says Kehoe made her take the job as the first women's athletic director in Maryland's department of intercollegiate athletics, a position she held until 1980.

Weller retired from Maryland following the 2002 season with 499 wins and 286 losses. She says when she graduated from Maryland, her major goal was to feel like she never worked a day in her life and to never be a prisoner of her possessions. "That way you can be more passionate about it," she said. Few Maryland legends pursued their Terp basketball careers with as much passion as Weller.

# VICKY BULLETT

Vicky Bullett was making quite a name for herself as a high school basketball player in Martinsburg, West Virginia in the early 1980s, but few of the big-time college programs knew much about her. Bullet made the varsity team as a freshman at Martinsburg Senior High School, averaged 35 points a game as a junior and was named a Parade High School All-American her senior season. A little family support, though, was needed to further Bullett's basketball career. Don Bullett, the oldest of Vicky's six brothers, was his sister's high school coach during her junior and senior years and often drove six hours round trip to take Vicky to practice for her AAU team.

The effort paid off. While playing for the AAU team in a tournament in New Mexico, Maryland head coach Chris Weller and an assistant coach saw her play for the first time. They had heard little about her. Weller had received an anonymous letter encouraging the coach to see Bullett play.

would think (a top recruit) was in there. After five or 10 minutes, I said, 'Let's get out of here. I don't want anyone else to see this girl.' (Tennessee head coach) Pat Summit and I were the only two coaches who really went after her. When she signed with Maryland, I told some friends of mine, 'I think we just signed the best post player in the country."

Bullet ultimately became Maryland's all-time leading scorer and one of four All-Americans in the program. She was a member of two U.S. Olympic teams and won a gold medal in the 1988 Summer Games in Seoul, South Korea.

Bullet joined the Terps a year after coach Chris Weller endured the worst season of her career to that point. Maryland finished 9-18, and Weller was wary about her team prior to the 1985-86 season. "I don't

## "We were growing. Even though we lost that N.C. State game, we were getting better as a team."

[VICKY BULLETT]

"She was a little overweight and she wasn't as flashy as some of the other people," Weller said in Maryland's student newspaper *The Diamondback* in 2003. Still, she saw potential in the player. "We were pretty highly ranked and when people would see coaches from the higher-ranked teams in a gym they think we are going to all of a sudden arrive at the top-10 level," she said in *The Diamondback* in November 1985. "I think we are a very good team, we are not a great team. We could be beaten by anybody right now. As it stands, we would not be competitive with the top 10 teams in the country."

Bullett sat out the season through December to concentrate on academics, and Maryland started the season with an 11-5 record, before losing six straight games, including five to ACC opponents. Maryland then won three of its last four games leading to the ACC tournament, but not without a reminder of their youth. The loss in those four games was by 24 points to N.C. State in the last home game of the season.

The performance perplexed Weller. "I understand when kids are young, they panic or back off early in the season," she said after the game. "But I don't understand it at this point in the season."

Using a full-court press that caused 20 turnovers, the fifth-seeded Terps avenged its two regular-season losses to State with a stunning 22-point first-round tournament win over the Wolfpack. Again using

the full-court press and aided by 27 points from freshman Deanna Tate, Maryland then beat Virginia by 24 points in a semifinal game. The Cavaliers had beaten Maryland by 26 points during their late-season losing streak.

Special Collections, University of Maryland Libraries

# WALT WILLIAMS

# "In a lot of those games, I didn't know I had 30 points until the end of the game."

[WALT WILLIAMS]

point, and playing as an off guard would relieve some of the pressure," he said.

Virginia coach Jeff Jones observed before the Terps game against the Cavaliers on January 29 that Williams's streak was more incredible because he was not an excessive shot taker. Williams tallied 33 points in the game. His most productive output during the streak was a career-high 39 points against Wake Forest.

"In a lot of those games, I didn't know I had 30 points until the end of the game," he said. "It wasn't something I was concentrating on. We didn't have the most talented team, but those guys took a lot pride when I scored 30 points. They set good picks. They believed in me."

Williams says the most profound memory of his Terps career occurred when he returned from the leg injury during his junior year on February 23 during Maryland's final home game of the season against Wake Forest. Maryland was 14-11 with three games remaining in their abbreviated season. Disallowed from the ACC tournament and a possible NCAA tournament berth due to the NCAA sanctions, Maryland was motivated to finish the season with a winning record.

Williams initially thought he would miss the entire rest of the season after the injury. But he received medical clearance to play two weeks before the game. He initially thought of playing in games once he was able

to run, but after talking to his mother and Maryland's coaches, all agreed he should not rush his return. Coach Williams left it up to Walt Williams to tell him when he was ready to play. Two days before the game, Coach Williams thought Walt Williams would be available only for an emergency situation, such as a free throw shooter or a final three-point shot.

When Williams decided to dress for the Wake Forest game, he thought that was an indication to the coach that he was ready to play, and that he would enter the game sometime early in the first half. But he never told Coach Williams he wanted in. Williams asked an assistant coach to tell Coach Williams that he wanted to play. The assistant told Walt Williams it would be best to tell the coach himself. He did so just before the teams returned for the second half. Coach Williams wanted to be sure that Walt Williams wasn't making a decision based too much on emotion since Maryland was losing the game.

The Terps trailed by four points with 13:23 remaining when Williams entered the game. Coach Williams said after the game that he tried to sneak him in with teammate Evers Burns, a forward. But when the two reported to the scorer's table to check in, the student section behind the scorer's table rose and cheered wildly. The rest of the

# GARY WILLIAMS

The first time I closely witnessed the maniacal game mannerisms of Gary Williams, I sat a few rows behind the Maryland bench in Cole Field House during a contest in the early 1990s. I was amazed at both how often he used profanity to make a point or express frustration and how anyone could portray that level of emotional intensity and not suffer some kind of breakdown.

The first time I met Gary Williams, the person, away from a competitive environment, I observed the antithesis of manic. I was promoting my first book, *Tales from the Maryland Terrapins*, at a live broadcast of Williams's radio show at the Green Turtle Restaurant in early January 2004. Before Williams went on the air, I approached him to say hello. We had talked several times on the phone—mostly for research for the book, and I had interviewed him for television after a game in the mid-1990s—but we had never met in a relaxed environment. He was personable, casually engaging, and sincere. I thanked him for cooperating with me for the book. He said he read the book and enjoyed it. I walked

## "There was never a kid who worked harder."

[BUD MILLIKAN]

away from the brief conversation surprised at his easygoing nature.

Emotionally reactive on the basketball court, passive and reflective away from the spotlight, Williams projects a compelling persona. Those traits have helped him accom-

plish more than any other Maryland basketball legend. Williams not only served a significant role as a player, he is also the first college coach since 1974 to lead his alma mater to a national basketball title.

Williams developed his trademark intensity playing the game as a youth in Collingswood, New Jersey. He used basketball in part to help him deal with his parents' divorce, an incident that developed in Williams a strong self-reliance that prevails today.

He writes in his book, *Sweet Redemption*, "Sports were a way to get an equal footing. Once you hit the court, it didn't matter who you were or what your family was like. You were either a player or not. ...I remember dragging home as a kid when it was getting dark after playing for hours and hours."

Williams was an all-state point guard at Collingswood High School who dreamed of playing college basketball in nearby Philadelphia, Pennsylvania. He had hoped to play at the University of Pennsylvania with a boyhood friend, but his grades were insufficient. After seeing Cole Field House for the first time, he picked Maryland over such schools as Clemson and Providence.

His exemplary work rate continued in College Park. "I know this—there was never a kid who worked harder," said his coach, Bud Millikan. "He was a quick learner, one of those guys in practice you'd have to build in some rest situations (in order to get him to take a break). Nobody should be able to go an entire practice at full speed. If he was on the floor, he was full bore."

Williams was a starter for Coach Millikan for three seasons and was the team captain during his senior campaign in 1967. He earned the reputation at Maryland as the quintessential point guard—feeding the ball often to players who were considered scorers, such as Jay McMillen, the Terps' leading scorer in 1965 and 1967, and Gary Ward, the top scorer in 1966. North Carolina head coach Dean Smith once said that Williams was "what a point guard should be."

He showed intensity both exuberantly and quietly. "He was kind of a classic point guard," said McMillen. "He wasn't the greatest scorer. He was serious about basketball, wasn't a screw off,

and had a good sense of humor. He was not loud and vociferous, and he had a quietness about him that was respected."

Billy Jones was part of a three-guard starting unit at times along with Williams and Pete Johnson.

"He was a hard-nosed player," said Jones. "We did a lot of trapping and worked hard in transition. Gary would bring the ball up the court and was unselfish. He was where he was supposed to be on the court."

Jones remembers one of the first times he witnessed Williams's intensity on the

Special Collections, University of Maryland Libraries

basketball court. As a freshman in early January, 1965, Jones sat in the first rows behind the Maryland bench to watch the Terps host a North Carolina team that featured future NBA Hall of Famer Billy Cunningham.

## "He was a hard-nosed player. He was where he was supposed to be on the court."

[BILLY JONES]

"(Coach) Bud (Millikan) called a timeout in the last two minutes of the game," said Jones. "You could see Gary was so intense. He didn't look at you when he talked. As they were going back on the floor, he was barking out orders, his fists clenched. He was hard-nosed. If you played pickup against Gary, you knew you had to work offensively to get a shot. Gary would be all over you. He coaches the way he played. Gary was always intense. That's nothing new."

Williams writes in his book, *Sweet Redemption*, that he left Maryland feeling bitter about his playing experience. He says he did not think Maryland cared about basketball. Maryland's assistant coach, Frank Fellows, worked part time as a University teacher and had to recruit players as well as teach and coach. Other ACC schools employed full-time assistant coaches. Williams lamented that basketball players could have been treated better at Maryland, especially compared to football players.

Williams's playing career at Maryland started well. In his sophomore season, Maryland finished 18-8 and tied for second place in the ACC regular season. It was the first winning season for Coach Millikan in four years. The Terps' biggest win was a three-point victory over fifth-ranked Duke in late February in Cole Field House.

But Williams's most fond moment as a Terp player took place during his junior season. The Terps traveled to New Orleans in late December to play in the Sugar Bowl Tournament. Its first-round opponent was Houston and the renowned Elvin Hayes, considered one of the best big men to ever play the game. Maryland beat Houston by one point, and then beat Dayton by two points the next night to win the tournament. It was a highlight in what was otherwise considered a disappointing season for a Maryland team that featured seven seniors and four juniors on the roster. Maryland had received a top-20 national ranking entering the season, but they finished with a 14-11 record and lost in the first round of the ACC tournament to North Carolina.

The unique talents of Hayes stand out when Williams reflects on the tournament.

"There weren't a lot of games on television then, so I wasn't sure how good Hayes was," he said. "But I remember how good he was. He was 6-10 and could shoot the ball. I remember going in for a lay-up—thought I had it for sure. But he came in and blocked it. You really saw why they were great. You experienced it yourself."

As a coach, Williams understandably is most fond of the NCAA title the Terps won in 2002.

"Nothing can match that," he said. "What made it really special were the feelings of the Maryland people, what it meant to them. When you play in a league with Duke and North Carolina, teams who have won it, sometimes you feel you're not as good as they are. It put us at their level."

Close behind the national title is the Terps' unlikely run to the 2004 ACC title. It was Williams's first ACC championship, and it took him 15 years to reach that pinnacle.

"For a lot of alumni, that was very important," he said. The tournament's been played 46 out of 50 years in North Carolina. To beat three Carolina teams in Greensboro, and beat the number one and three seeds, that was special."

## "He coaches the way he played. Gary was always intense. That's nothing new."

[BILLY JONES]

# JOE
# SMITH

# KEITH
# BOOTH

The 1995-96 Maryland basketball season was one of the most disappointing of Gary Williams's coaching career. The Terps returned four starters from a team that was ACC regular-season co-champions and reached the NCAA Tournament Sweet Sixteen. Maryland received a number-14 preseason ranking. But after seven games, Maryland fell from the national rankings, and the Terps finished the season with a 17-13 record after losing in the first round of the NCAA Tournament.

By contrast, little was expected of the Terps' 1996-97 team. Keith Booth was the only starter who returned from the previous season. *The Diamondback* called the Terps—who were picked to finish eighth in the conference—"too young, too small and too bad to compete in the ACC." But the Terps put together one of the more rewarding seasons under Coach Williams.

Booth developed into the player Maryland fans had hoped for after the high school All-American from Baltimore's Dunbar High School had agreed to play in College Park. Playing his first two years in the surprising shadow of classmate Joe Smith, Booth averaged 10 points per game in both his freshman and sophomore seasons, and was the Terps' second leading rebounder, behind Smith, during his second year. Booth was also the team's second leading scorer and the leading rebounder during his junior year, and was an all-ACC pick each of his four years.

By most accounts, Booth's senior season was a pleasant surprise. Maryland won their first 11 games, tying the 1975-76 team for the best start to a season. After Maryland beat 10th-ranked Duke in late January, Maryland

reached it's best national ranking of the season, at number five. After a loss to Florida State in its next game, Maryland boasted a 17-3 record and finished the year at 9-7 in the ACC, in a tie for fourth place.

Booth recalls Maryland's sixth win of the season as his most memorable moment as a Terp. Maryland entered the final game of the Franklin National Bank Classic on a bit of a roll. After an 80-64 win over California in the tournament semifinal, Maryland fell behind 16-4 at the start of the tournament final against George Washington University, a 5-2 team that was ranked 26th in the country, four spots ahead of Maryland.

Maryland struggled early against George Washington's zone defense. But the Terps turned the game around with a pressing defense and a dynamic transition game. Behind Booth's nine points, Maryland led 34-29 at the half.

With the Colonial's big men in foul trouble, Booth took an aggressive approach to the second half.

"It was a situation where somebody had to step up," he said after the game. "People were in foul trouble. So I knew I could take

# "No recruit was more important than Keith Booth."

[COACH GARY WILLIAMS]

the ball to the hole aggressively and not be challenged."

Booth's assertive nature netted him 20 points in the second half. He made 16 of 24 free throws in the game, and his 29 points were a career best. A stretch late in the game showcased Booth's dominance. With 4:55 left and Maryland up by four, Booth took an outlet pass after Maryland blocked a shot. He drove to the basket against two Colonial players and was fouled while executing a swooping lay-up. Booth missed the free throw, but grabbed the rebound and was fouled driving to the basket. He made one of two free throws to put Maryland up by seven.

Booth also grabbed 12 rebounds, and the Terps won 74-68. His performance prompted the following praise from Gary Williams.

"Keith Booth is one of the 10 best seniors in the country without a doubt," Williams said after the game. "I read all the preseason magazines and newspapers and nowhere did I find Keith Booth as one of the top seniors. He should get the recognition he deserves."

Booth ultimately did. In his senior season, Booth was a third-team All-America pick and a consensus All-ACC first-team selection. He also received two votes for ACC Player of the Year. Booth holds the school record for free throws made in a career (576) and a season (213 in 1997). Booth also started every game Maryland played during his four years at the school.

More importantly than his awards and impressive numbers, Booth helped sustain a program that was still struggling to again gain consistent national recognition. Terps coach Gary Williams credits two people for having the most impact in turning around his program: Walt Williams and Keith Booth. Williams stayed at Maryland after the program received probation in 1989 for violations committed when Bob Wade was head coach. Williams departed Maryland as the school record holder in scoring average for a season (26.8 in 1992) and an All-American.

Booth picked Maryland over Kentucky and Duke, among others, at a time when recruits from Baltimore generally ignored Maryland.

"He was told by people from his community that he wouldn't get treated right," said Gary Williams. "Him coming to Maryland opened up the eyes of other players from Baltimore to come to Maryland."

One was Rodney Elliot, who entered Maryland one year after Booth and played four years for the Terps. Another was Juan Dixon, who helped lead Maryland to a national championship as a senior in 2002.

In his book, *Sweet Redemption*, Williams commented on Keith Booth's significance to Maryland's basketball program:

"No recruit was more important than Keith Booth. ...You can be talented and good, but you have to be tough, too. Keith allowed us to get tough as a program. Keith had to be very tough because there were people very upset about him coming to Maryland. ... Once

> ## "One of the things I always say is that I really feel very fortunate to have been a big part of helping turn the program around."
>
> [KEITH BOOTH]

he was here and playing ball, he would throw his body at people. He was not a great shooter, but he would get knocked down a lot. Keith would bother some people so that they would try and knock him down. He liked that. And he would make two free throws and hammer the guy again. He put his toughness into our program for four years."

Booth says he's most proud of helping to revive Maryland's program.

"One of the things I always say is that I really feel very fortunate to have been a big part of helping turn the program around," Booth said recently in *The Diamondback.* "When I first got here, you couldn't go into a store and really find any Maryland stuff. Now, everywhere you go, you can find a Maryland hat or T-shirt."

Booth was a first-round pick in the 1997 draft by the Chicago Bulls, which won an NBA championship in 1998, Booth's second and final year in the NBA. Through the spring of 2004, Booth worked at the Park School in Baltimore. He returned to Maryland's bench for the 2004 season as an assistant coach for the Terps.

# STEVE FRANCIS

J.J. BUSH

As an athletic trainer at a major university, J.J. Bush's main job is to help heal the broken and bruised bodies of elite athletes. But Bush found in his over three decades as a trainer at Maryland that his role stretches far beyond ice packs and taped ankles.

Bush, similar to most athletic trainers, has unique access to athletes and coaches when they can be at their most emotionally vulnerable. It happens during quiet times of reflection for an athlete during solitary time spent rehabilitating an injury, or for a coach who needs someone with whom to calmly chat, away from the hectic demands of the season, and during private group moments of celebration or dejection.

As the longest tenured active trainer in the Atlantic Coast Conference, during his 32 years on the job Bush has had primary access to the inner happenings of an athletic department. And no other incident stands out for the Maryland basketball legend as memorably as an event that took place on March 13, 1994. On that day, the Maryland men's basketball team gathered in the team meeting room near the Terps' locker room in the lower levels of Cole Field House to watch the CBS network's broadcast of the NCAA Tournament selection show. Maryland had not played in the tournament since 1988 under second-year coach Bob Wade. In 1989, Gary Williams took over as head coach of a program that quickly fell into the abyss of NCAA sanctions. With limited television appearances and restricted access to postseason tournaments, Maryland basketball found itself mired in mediocrity.

Until the 1993-94 season, when freshman sensation Joe Smith and classmate Keith

Booth, along with a trio of sophomores—Exree Hipp, Johnny Rhodes and Duane Simpkins—helped Maryland achieve a national top-25 ranking for the first time since 1985. With a 14-11 record following the ACC tournament (8-8 in the ACC, for fourth place), Maryland was perched precariously on the tournament fence, hoping to fall gleefully on the side of participation.

> "The vast majority of coaches are control people. They need to have control over every aspect of their job."
>
> [J.J. BUSH]

When Maryland was announced as the 54th team picked in the field of 64 that year, as a number-10 seed in the Midwest Region, coach Gary Williams was brought to tears. Williams choked on his words as he talked to the media soon after the announcement was made. He said then he didn't know if he was prepared for not getting into the tournament.

"I could see the relief in Gary's face," said Bush, who was in the room with the team when the announcement was made. "The burden of the mess that he inherited

# "Lefty and I didn't see eye to eye on a lot of things."

[J.J. BUSH]

was finally lifted off of his back. I think the reason that particular moment stood out was the fact that Gary gave up a good situation at Ohio State. Then things happened here that he wasn't planning on happening. So all of this stuff is on top of (his) shoulders, and now we get a bid to go to the NCAA tournament and all of that garbage is lifted off and thrown away. Now he could breathe again, so to speak."

A graduate of Florida State, Bush came to Maryland in 1972 as an assistant trainer as a 25-year-old who had reached the rank of second lieutenant in the U.S. Army. He immediately began working with the men's basketball team, a job he endured for four seasons. With Driesell, Bush was part of an ACC regular season championship team in 1975, and helped such Maryland basketball legends as Tom McMillen, Len Elmore and John Lucas. But most memories of his time with Driesell focused on friction and struggle.

"I'm an airborne ranger, feeling pretty good about myself and think I know what's going on," he said. "Lefty and I didn't see eye to eye on a lot of things."

A point of contention was Bush's moustache, which he had worn since leaving the army in 1972. As the 1976 season approached, coach Driesell required that the men's basketball staff be clean-shaven. Bush's reluctance to part with his moustache prompted a meeting with athletic director Jim Kehoe.

"He said, 'Let me tell you this. If you get into an argument with the head coach, you're going to lose,'" said Bush. "I was smart enough to figure out where he was coming from. I went home and shaved my moustache."

Bush said Driesell fired Bush after he showed up the next preseason with the moustache back on his face. "The vast majority of coaches are control people," said Bush. "They need to have control over every aspect of their job."

Bush then worked as head trainer for Maryland's football team from 1976 to 1992 and was a part of four ACC titles. After athletic director Andy Geiger replaced Bush as the head trainer for football, Bush approached Gary Williams and said he'd like to work with the basketball team. Williams took Bush on, and he's been with the basketball team ever since.

During the 1993-94 season, Bush enjoyed one of his most gratifying experiences as an athletic trainer. During his freshman season the year before, guard Johnny Rhodes was one of the Terps' best defenders. His 71 steals that season ties him for most steals as a Terps freshman along with Steve Blake. Rhodes was bothered that year with a torn cartilage in a knee, an injury leftover from high school that Bush says Rhodes had not been able to treat properly.

Juan Dixon

# 2002
# NCAA CHAMPS

Steve Blake

Maryland Athletics Media Relations

year-old brother Kevin had been shot and killed in Houston the previous day. Mouton went home to Louisiana for the funeral.

Mouton possessed the Terps' most outgoing personality. Late in the season, Tahj Holden said of Mouton, "I always ask him, 'Mouton, why are you smiling?' and he says, 'Because I'm happy.' Then I ask, 'What are you happy for?' And he says, 'I don't know. I'm happy that I woke up.'"

## "[Blake] makes that engine go."

### [MATT DOHERTY]

Mouton was also happy to be a Terp. He transferred from Tulane after leading them in scoring during his freshman and sophomore seasons. His playing time had dipped as a sophomore, and he wanted a change of scenery. Mouton started the 2000-01 season on the Terps bench, but after the team's 1-3 start, Williams plugged him into the starting lineup, and the Terps went on a 10-game win streak. Mouton was a perfect role player on a team that had plenty of stars.

Mouton returned from Louisiana in time for the Terps' next game six days later against Detroit. Less than seven minutes into the contest, a standing ovation in Cole Field House greeted him as he came off the bench. The Terps won easily, 79-54, and Mouton finished with 13 points.

After edging N.C. State in their conference opener, the Terps rolled to a 112-79 victory over North Carolina, the most lopsided game of the 78-year-old rivalry. Blake recorded a career-high 14 assists in the win.

Maryland then faced top-ranked Duke. The Terps stayed close through the first half and received a boost before halftime from a surprising source. Randle, a six-foot-nine, 245-pound forward who had spent the previous two seasons at a junior college, was part of Gary Williams' eight-man rotation in his first year with the Terps. But he was only averaging about four points per game during his junior season. Randle scored seven points in the final 1:48 of the first half to put the Terps ahead by a point at halftime. Still, Duke pulled away for a 99-78 win. It was the Terps' last regular-season loss.

After winning their next three games by an average margin of 17 points, the Terps faced number-eight Virginia, which led by nine points with 3:22 to go. Maryland responded with 13 of the next 15 points. Junior Drew Nicholas, among the ACC leaders in scoring in 2003, was merely another of the Terps' role players in 2001-02. A smooth shooter, he had been patient for his opportunities, such as the one that presented itself against Virginia. Nicholas connected on two three-pointers—his first baskets of the game—to bring the Terps to within a point. Dixon then converted a baseline jumper to give the Terps the lead in a 91-87 win.

The momentum was building for a rematch with Duke. Late in the Terps' 85-65 win against Georgia Tech, a sold-out Cole Field House crowd began chanting, "We want Duke."

In the previous meeting between the two teams, Jayson Williams had torched Maryland for 34 points, but he would not be a factor this time. Steve Blake made sure of that, defending the All-American to six-of-

22 shooting and sapping the life out of the Blue Devils with a heads-up play before halftime. With the first half winding down and Duke in control of the ball, Williams turned to look back toward coach Mike Krzyzewski. As he did, Blake swooped in for the steal and converted a layup for a 38-29 lead.

"I just told myself if he does it again, I'm going to go after it," Blake said after the game of taking the ball from Williams at the end of the first half. "He turned again, so I just took off."

Blake was also a factor on the offensive end, recording 13 assists to only one turnover. Wilcox added a career-high 23 points and 11 rebounds in Maryland's 87-73 win.

During the next game in a win against Clemson, Dixon reached yet one more milestone in his improbable career. He became the first player in NCAA history to collect 2,000 points, 300 steals and 200 three-pointers. Before the next game against Wake Forest, Dixon and Baxter had their jerseys raised to the Cole Field House rafters, placing them among the greatest players to ever wear a Maryland uniform.

But Baxter and Dixon weren't just honorees that night. They were the main event. Baxter paced the Terps with 25 points and eight rebounds as the team fought off a 12-point second-half deficit to take the lead in the final two minutes. With the game tied at 89 and time about to expire, Wake Forest's Josh Howard snared a Dixon miss and immediately signaled for a timeout. But the Demon Deacons had already used all their timeouts, resulting in a technical foul. With 1.2 seconds left, Dixon stepped to the line and sunk the game-winning free throw for a 90-89 win.

At the final home game against Virginia—also the last men's game played at 47-year-old Cole Field House—Maryland beat Virginia, 112-92, ending the season 15-0 at home and clinching the program's first ACC regular-season championship since 1980. Maryland shot 72.7 percent in the second half against Virginia. Six Maryland players, led by Dixon's 23 points, scored in double figures. Wilcox had 21 points and 11 rebounds, Baxter had 20 points and eight rebounds, and Blake added 15 points and 10 assists. The last points at Cole were scored, though, by little-used freshman Andre Collins on a three-pointer in the final seconds.

Afterward, the players and Gary Williams took turns cutting down the net nearest to the Maryland bench. Dixon cut off the last chord before realizing his coach had yet to take his turn. Dixon tied the last piece of net back on for Williams, who made the final snip.

Maryland roared into the ACC tournament on a 12-game winning streak. But Maryland lost to N.C. State in the semifinals, 86-82. Still, the Terps received their first NCAA Tournament No. 1 seed in program history.

But the loss to N.C. State created concern among the team. "One of our team's goals was to win the ACC title," Mike Grinnon said. "Losing that put us back into place."

Dixon called a players-only meeting in a cramped hotel room on the eve of the Terps' NCAA Tournament first-round game against heavy-underdog Sienna. "He said, 'There's nothing going to stop us,'" Grinnon said. "I

Lonny Baxter

# POETIC
# JUSTICE

Many Maryland players not profiled in this book have performed legendary acts. Here is a tribute to some of those efforts:

*Chances are you didn't see*
*when Al Bunge scored his 43.*
*He did it January 4, 1960.*
*It's second all-time behind Ernie G.*

*From the free throw line, he had a plan,*
*this sharpshooter Jerry Greenspan.*
*14 of 14 made in one game,*
*no other Terp can claim that fame.*

*Will Hetzel's shot from 40 feet*
*beat the buzzer, what a treat.*
*The Dukies lost by just two,*
*Lefty's alma mater, the Terps took it to you.*

*They carried Lefty away,*
*the ride was not short,*
*he flashed the "V", the king and his court.*
*For the first time, it happened then,*
*that glorious sound, "Aaa-men."*

*Jimmy O'Brien made it quite untame,*
*against South Carolina in the slow-down game.*
*With five seconds left his shot goes in,*
*into O.T. they go, for the win.*

*Their previous game ended in a fight,*
*but not on this crazy night.*
*With four seconds left his shot goes in,*
*a 31-30 wild Maryland win.*

Earnest Graham set the record straight,
on December 20, 1978.
Forty-four points against N.C. State,
in one game, no other Terp's been so great.

For Terps fans, no reason to gripe
when Greg Manning stepped to the charity stripe.
.858 for a career, in one year .908,
no other Terp's been so great.

From the field, Greg really could see,
the season's best .643, set in '80.
Along with Matt Roe, books were their friends.
They and Tom Mac—Academic All-Americans.

Ben Coleman showed that he could score,
he led the team in '84.
Off the boards, too, he was tops.
That year he was hard to stop.

The Terps won the ACC tourney,
ending a surprising journey.
That year he made All-ACC,
as he did in '83.

Down in Chapel Hill, the Dean Dome shocked.
Jeff Baxter's 20-footer beat the clock.
Lenny took charge with dunks, jumpers, blocks, steals.
An O.T. win that was so surreal.

Keith Gatlin wanted to ice the cake.
A pass off Kenny Smith's back was no fake.
From out of bounds, he caught the ball,
made the layup, it's over, that's all.

*The Lewis boys knew how to play,*
*from the basket, they'd keep the ball away.*
*They led the Terps in swats per game,*
*Cedric and Derrick, a dozen blocks brought you fame.*

*For the season, Derrick's ahead,*
*in '91, 143 shots went dead.*
*Cedric leads the career tally,*
*he sent 339 to no-point alley.*

*He's the king of swipes, no debating there,*
*John Rhodes is tops, 344 in a career.*
*His best number came in '96,*
*110 for the year; vs. Carolina, nine picks.*

*That clever guard Terrell Stokes*
*knew how to upset opposing folks.*
*15 assists vs. W. Carolina in '98,*
*in one game, no other Terp's been so great.*

*Duane Simpkins and Terrell, also Kevin Mac*
*consistently built the Terps' attack.*
*Three straight years, they led their teams*
*in assists; they were a shooter's dream.*

*As a freshman, no one was as great,*
*as lightning-quick guard Deanna Tate,*
*Averaged 16.7 points a game,*
*and was destined for unparalleled fame.*

*She missed the next year due to injury,*
*but came back to play with intensity.*
*She's fifth on the all-time scoring list,*
*an All-American, who was missed.*

Kris Kirchner scored 39 in one game,
that all-time best is her fame.
But she made some fans shed some tears,
when she left the Terps after three years.

A big man with lots of tricks,
he was All-ACC, in '55 and '56.
He led the Terps in rebounding and scoring,
big Bob Kessler was rarely boring.

He led the Terps in scoring, and his D was fine.
Laron Profit made All-ACC, '97 to '99,
his career best was 32, as a senior against FSU.
He's third all-time in career steals;
Laron was the real deal.

Jerrod Mustaf came in strong,
but he wasn't here too long.
A top scorer and 'bounder his first year,
third-team All-ACC, let's spread the cheer.

Against fourth-ranked Duke, he scored 35,
but Terps lose in o.t., a good try.
After two years, he went away
to a four-year career in the NBA.

Tony Massenburg played with Jerrod
and over his teammate he got the nod.
In the ACC tourney he made first team,
something Jerrod could only dream.
But like his mate, being a third-team ACC pick
certainly didn't make him sick.
In the NBA, he's had some fun,
with 13 teams since '91.

Terence Morris, from Frederick,
became a three-time All-ACC pick.
He's top 10 all time in scoring points,
he'd shoot from wide, down low and the point.

He was pretty strong on the boards,
number five all time is his reward.
His senior year was quite a tour;
he helped the Terps to the Final Four.

Who can forget the masterful run?
The 2004 team, they made it fun.
Winning the ACC tourney,
sent Terps fans to interminable glee.

Jamar Smith, he brought his game
after a time when it was just too tame.
Johnny G, he stole the show,
The opponents could just say "d'oh".

Mike Grinnon stepped to the line,
with a lot at stake, he did just fine.

D.J, Ekene, Hassan, Jones and Bowers,
The group of frosh had their finest hours.
Travis, Nik, Darien and Chris Mac,
They all helped sustain a winning attack.

I hope I've honored all who were,
deserving of such praising verse.
If I've omitted a player who's worthy,
Apologies to all, hey, I'm just a guy from Jersey.

# Celebrate the Heroes of College Basketball
## in These Other Releases from Sports Publishing!

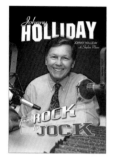

**Johnny Holliday: From Rock to Jock**
by Johnny Holliday with Stephen Moore
Foreword by Tony Kornheiser

• 6 x 9 hardcover
• 225+ pages
• 8-page b/w photo section
• $22.95

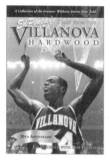

**Ed Pinckney's Tales from the Villanova Hardwood**
by Ed Pinckney with Bob Gordon

• 5.5 x 8.25 hardcover
• 200 pages
• b/w photos throughout
• $19.95
• 2004 Release!

**Tales from the Wake Forest Hardwood**
by Dan Collins

• 5.5 x 8.25 hardcover
• 200 pages
• b/w photos throughout
• $19.95
• 2004 Release!

**One Hundred Years of Duke Basketball: A Legacy of Achievement**
by Bill Brill

• 8.5 x 11 hardcover • 240+ pp
• photos throughout
• $29.95 • 2004 Release!

**Tales from the Maryland Terrapins**
by David Ungrady

• 5.5 x 8.25 hardcover
• 200 pages
• b/w photos throughout
• $19.95

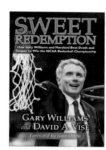

**Sweet Redemption**
by Gary Williams with David A. Vise

• 6 x 9 hardcover
• 250 pages
• 8-page b/w photo section
• $24.95

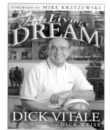

**Dick Vitale's Living a Dream**
by Dick Vitale with Dick Weiss

• 6 x 9 hardcover
• 250 pages
• 16-page color photo section
• $24.95 • 2004 Release!

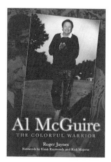

**Dick Enberg: Oh My! 50 Years of Rubbing Shoulders with Greatness**
by Dick Enberg with Jim Perry

• 6 x 9 hardcover
• 250 pages
• 16-page b/w photo section
• $24.95 • 2004 Release!

**Al McGuire: The Colorful Warrior**
by Roger Jaynes

• 6 x 9 hardcover
• 275+ pages
• 8-page b/w photo section
• $24.95
• 2004 Release!

**Terps: National Champions (2002)**
by The Baltimore Sun

• 8.5 x 11 hard/softcover
• 160 pages
• color photos throughout
• $19.95 (softcover)
• $29.95 (hardcover)